Can I Tell You My Side?

Poetry From A Mother's Heart

Can I Tell You My Side?

Poetry From A Mother's Heart

MARY ANN HARRING-DUHART

ARPress

ILLUMINATING IDEAS
EMPOWERING VOICES

ARPress
45 Dan Road Suite 5
Canton MA 02021

Hotline:1(888) 821-0229
Fax:1(508) 545-7580

Ordering Information:
Quantity sales. Special discounts are available on quantity purchases by corporations, associations, and others. For details, contact the publisher at the address above.

Printed in the United States of America.
ISBN-13:   Paperback   979-8-89330-240-0
              eBook   979-8-89330-239-4

Library of Congress Control Number: 2024901458

My Acknowledgements

To my Lord and Savior Jesus Christ who inspired me to start venting my pains in poetry.

And we know that all things work together for good to them that love God, to them who are the called according to *his* purpose. Romans 8:28

My spouse- Verdell Duhart Jr. who has supported and critiqued my work from time to time. For this is our story and it is All to the Glory of God.

To my sons-Michael Dixon and wife, Amy Dixon, Bryant, Vernon, Andre', and Nathaniel Duhart.

A special thank you to my dear co-worker Connie Rice who has inspired me to continue to write. She is my angel now and I can hear her say "I get the first copy."

To all of my brothers and sisters, my poetry soup friends, and my viewing audience for your words of encouragement, prayers, and continuing pushing me to write-write-write. You all know who you are and I do thank you.

To My Pastor Orvelester Strassner and wife, Judith Strassner. The Eastside COGIC Church Family who has also kept me in their prayers and supported me in my endeavors and held me during the storms of life. Thank you all for your love and continual support. Thank you-Thank you-Thank You.

To my new publishers at Author Reputation Press- thank you for discovering me and helping me to bring back to my reading audience "Can I Tell You My Side-Poetry from a Mother's Heart."

Introduction

A comment was sent to me one day from a reviewer reading my poetry.

He stated, "Mary I never knew the pain I put my mother through until I read your work" (poetry). That statement has stayed in my heart and it has helped me to see and grasp the purpose behind writing. For I am learning daily, it is not about me but Him, God. He has a way of getting His word out. I am just so thankful that I can be the vessel *for such a time as this. (Esther 4:14).*

Over the last four years the Lord has taken my life on a new journey. That journey is poetry. I have taken no formal writing classes. I am inspired by the Lord to write. I don't write daily but by His leading and by life experiences. I believe by doing it this way I can truly say, "The hand of the Lord has done this." Man gets no glory, it all belongs to God.

I pray as you read Can I Tell You My Side you will find healing and encouragement in the words of these poems.

I would like to also thank you in advance for hearing *my side of the story...*

Can I Tell You My Side?

One day I heard my sister say, "There's two sides to every Story."

Can I tell you my side- so that God can get the Glory?

I just want to share with you my testimony you see.

For there are readers reading me that have a special need.

As I release the pain I feel by writing things out-

I often read of your response and it makes me want to shout.

So can I tell you my side by writing line by line?

Can I take you on my journey-one poem at a time!

CONTENTS

Finding Purpose

I may not be able to write these poems in poetic forms like you.
Many times, my English may sound broken in bits and pieces too.
But there's a message in my heart that I would like to share.
Whoever reads these poems knows that someone out there cares.

The message is not in rhythm and flow as some readers seek.
It is not in fancy words or lines that sound so deep.
The message is so simple that it will prick the heart.
If it reaches just one soul I know I have done my part.

The Lord will get the Glory out of all that is said and done.
Even through these writings I know a soul is won.
As I read the comments that have come my way-
I am finding purpose in writing from day to day.

I Had to Go Through It

I had to go through it
There was no place to escape.
The storms that came at me
Was certainly no mistake.

I had to go through it
I had to feel the pain.
Otherwise I would not have any compassion.
For others going through the rain.

"I had to go through it."
I heard the preacher say.
How can I find my purpose
If I don't know how to pray?

I had to go through it.
My name was at the top of the test.
I must lead the way for others
So they can learn how to lean on Him and find rest.

I had to go through it.
This was my cross I had to bear.
So many are searching for answers.
I must be able to share.

I had to go through it.
It was certainly no fault of mine.
I was minding my own business.
When this storm began to ride.

I Had To Go Through It!!!

A State of Contentment

You never know what life will bring.
Some things happen that may cause you to sing.
Then other things may cause you to sigh-
Only the Lord knows the reason why.

Trapped in a bus terminal with nothing to do.
Listening to others singing the blues.
On my way home from another state-
Caught in a snowstorm- this is great!

The winds are blowing strong, so it is very cold.
Highway forty has now been closed.
Listening to the voices coming from all around.
Their stories are so scary it makes you want to frown.

So in the meantime I will keep a smile.
Until it's time to go that extra mile.
Then we will be back on the road again.
Trying to reach our destination and
Connect with the family one more time.

Still My Son

When he chooses to run away-
He is still my son.

When he chooses to curse at me-
He is still my son.

When he chooses to drop out of school-
He is still my son.

When he chooses to use alcohol and drugs-
He is still my son.

When he chooses to run with the wrong friends-
He is still my son.

When he chooses not to serve the God I serve-
He is still my son.

When spouse and church family don't understand-
He is still my son.

If he gets locked up for his mistakes-
He is still my son.

A mother's love is unconditional.
I'm learning this day by day.

I birthed this son into the world and
Have loved him all the way.

The choices that he may decide to make,
May seem like Greek to me.
There will be more days to come,
When we may never agree.

I will continue to love and pray for him
Until my life on earth is done.
God gave this child to me and
He will forever be-My Son!

Where Are Our Sons?

Sitting and pondering don't know which way to go.
Where are our sons we really would like to know?
Left the house the other day and did not say a word.
It's been days now and we still have not even heard.

Where are our sons? We really would like to know.
What are they into out in the world so cold?
Wandering the streets from day to day we just don't have a clue.
We just don't understand and our hearts are feeling blue.

Doesn't they understand a mother's aching heart?
Can't they feel the pain we feel when we are apart?
Many sleepless nights we have when they're not in the house.
Where are our sons? Where are their where abouts?

Father where are our son, we really would like to know.
We just don't understand why did they have to go?
Why do they choose to run the streets from night to night?
Can someone please tell me-
Why can't they do the things that's right?

How Do You Pray?

How do you pray for a son that's run-away?
Wandering the streets from day to day,
What is a mother supposed to say?

How do you pray for a son that running with unknown friends?
Friends in trouble with the law and can't find no peace within.

How do you pray for a son that's robbing folks blind?
"Thumping"- is what they call it in this day and time.

How do you pray when you can't find that peace of mind?
Thinking about your children during these perilous times.

How do you pray when you just can't seem to find a prayer?
You know there is an answer- you know the answer is out there.

Invisible Tears

Shedding profoundly behind the heart.
Where no man can see them from the very start.
Putting on a facade from day to day.
Not even thinking about what others have to say.

Invisible tears never seen by man.
But deep down within you can feel the pain.
Tears that can't be seen by the human eyes.
Flooding the soul so deep down inside.

Invisible tears shed day after day.
While watching your children who have gone astray.
They're hanging out with friends who aren't so bright.
Roaming in the streets night after night.

Invisible tears that are silently seen.
While on the inside you just want to scream.
Invisible tears who can wipe them away?
At this very moment all I can do is pray.

A Mother's Plea

I was never given a manual on how to be a parent.
In this 21st century it really doesn't matter.
Raising teenage sons with such a stubborn will.
I find it hard to master and the challenge isn't thrilling.

I'm faced with generational curses from day to day.
Many sleepless nights I find it so hard to pray.
I often ask myself, "where did things go wrong?"
I thought I gave the orders not take them from my sons.

As I sat at home and watch the path they take.
I just say a prayer and hope it's not to late.
I ask for ministering angels to surround my sons.
Minister to their spirit and show them where they're wrong.

I ask for God's protection as they run life out on the streets.
Please shield them from all harm for their souls are very weak.
I pray that someone special will come into their lives.
Please send a special mentor to show them what is right.

From the Soul of a Mother

Deep down within my heart is this terrible pain.
As I look upon my children standing out in the rain.
Without an umbrella nor a coat upon their backs.
Wandering this world of sin and ignoring all of the facts.

Night after night they stay away,
All I can do is pray.
Walking the floors night after night.
Hoping one day they will see and come to the light.

The thunders roar- the lightening flash-
My heart flutters with so much fear.
I can't find rest from night to night
As long as my children aren't near.

The tears flow hard as the days go by
And still the children are gone.
The tears flow like a broken day
As this mother buries her soul.

No Easy Task

It's not easy being a parent in these last and evil days.
I often sit and wonder, why are things this way?
The choices that my children make are all like Greek to me.
I cry and pray from day to day looking for relief.

There was a time when you could lay things down-
And later pick them up.
Now things and money have taken legs and
All I can do is fuss.
I've lost my trust in what they say and can't believe a word.
This awful feeling is deep within and
I feel like I'm in another world.

Lord I know you will not give me more than I can bear.
But sometimes I feel like I'm on overload and
I need someone to share.
I ask for strength from day to day to make it through the night.
Lord I need your guidance- for I must not lose this fight.

Somebody's Child

Somebody's child have lost their way.
Wandering the streets from day to day.
Stealing to satisfy their fleshly needs
That's Somebody's Child oh can't you see.

Somebody's child is searching for love.
In all the wrong places on this earth below.
Heads bowed low and can't see their way.
That's somebody's child who has gone astray.

Somebody's child is living in fear.
Drowning their sorrows in a river of tears.
Self-esteem low and don't even care.
That's somebody's child that need our prayers.

Somebody's child is carrying a gun.
They are hurting others and living on the run.
Thinking that they are tough with their malicious deeds.
That's Somebody's Child and we must intercede.

The Fight

I birthed four sons into this world and I gave them life.
When two of them reached their teens they decided to take a flight.
Not on a plane, train, or bus you see
But into a world of gangs, thieves, alcohol and weed.

Day by day I cried and cried and didn't know what to do.
The world had captured two of my sons what was I supposed to do.
I prayed and prayed to seek God's face with each new passing day.
I asked the Lord for strength from above to overcome what may.

The road has not been easy but yet I keep going on.
I know within my heart that I have taught them right from wrong.
I am fighting in a battle and sometimes it seems so hard to see.
These strongholds must be broken so that my children can be set free.

Fighting it in my own strength is certainly not enough.
If it was left up to me I would curse and fuss.
But I know that's not the answer to this problem that is so deep.
I must take it to my Father for we are all His sheep.

Our children all belong to Him I know that this is true.
He loaned them to us for a while to show them what to do.
They will make mistakes at times as they are learning how to grow.
We must keep them in our prayers until the days grow old.

A Tearful Good-Bye

How do you say good-bye to a child that is so young.
The memories of yesterday when everything went wrong.
As we look upon your picture of the shell that is lying there.
It grieves our hearts and makes us think that life is just not fair.

Although the Lord knew what He was doing it still makes it
Hard to accept.
Sometimes it's hard to handle all the things that life has dealt.
A body so frail and tender had just began to form.
No one could comprehend that you would leave with so much harm.

A nightmare imbedded within our heads of that terrible night.
When a little one left this earth without no one in sight.
Things that happened in the dark is now coming into the light.
We pray that the final outcome will make everything alright.

Your little life touched so many hearts as you walked upon this earth.
Although it was cut short the Father knew this from your birth.
The Angels came to rescue you from the environment that you were in.
So safely in our Father's arms you are resting once again.

Tears and Prayers

He turned seventeen on yesterday.
About two years ago he ran away.
I didn't understand why all went wrong.
Why did he run into someone else's arms?

I birthed this son into the world.
One day he left home without a care.
Didn't even bother to say good-bye.
All I could do was cry, cry, cry.

Night after night I shed rivers of tears.
Trying to understand a mother's fear.
Kept asking the Lord why were these things so?
Deep down within I had to let him go.

This new generation I don't understand.
What's going on? What's in the plan.
I asked the Lord this time after time.
Is He silent or am I losing my mind.

I know one day I will plainly see.
So in the meantime I will stay on my knees.
I will continue to pray for he is yet my son.
With the help of the Lord this battle will be won.

Another Fight with Death

There came a knock upon the door.
A young man stood with his head bowed low.
Coming over to bear bad news.
Your son's in the hospital and looking blue.

We were drinking ma'am you see.
Your son drunk to such a degree.
To much drinking is not good.
Family in limbo and don't know what to do.

Fighting with strongholds on this very day.
Praying and praying and don't know what to say.
Lost in the process and looking for peace of mind.
A mother's heart is aching one more time.

Crying out for answer during these perilous times.
Fighting a spiritual battle and trying to stand my ground.
In the meantime I will stay upon my knees.
I am also asking for friends to stand in agreement with me.

How Do You Pray (Revised)

How do you pray for a son that's run-away?
Wandering the streets from day to day,
What is a mother supposed to say?

How do you pray for a son that running with unknown friends?
Friends in trouble with the law and can't find no peace within.

How do you pray for a son that's robbing folks blind?
"Thumping"- is what they call it in this day and time.

How do you pray when you can't find that peace of mind?
Thinking about your children during these perilous times.

How do you pray when you just can't seem to find a prayer?
You know there is an answer- you know the answer is out there.

You pray for God's protection each and every day.
You pray the He would send Angels to minister to them in some way.
You pray for peace of mind and comfort for your soul.
You pray for the Lord's Leading for He certainly knows what's in store.

What Do You Do?

What do you do when your heart is feeling blue?
Searching for answers and you just don't have a clue.
What do you do?

What do you do when you feel all hope is gone?
Children still leaving and moving from home to home.
What do you do?

What do you do when you don't know what to do?
Feels like I'm marking time and I don't know what else to do.
What do you do?

What do you do keeps ringing in my ears.
Living with the unknown makes a mother fear.
What do you do?

Stop and take a moment- whisper a silent prayer.
Our Father knows the answer and He will not leave you in despair.

A Mother's Request

I'm looking at this demon and I don't know what to do.
Fighting a massive stronghold and it's pulling my heart into.
Stealing from their loved ones to help them supply their need.
Their bodies are crying out for more weed, weed, weed.

This old ugly demon gets stronger by the day.
As I look upon their faces, all I can do is pray.
Praying for deliverance for my teenage sons.
It seems like a losing battle,
But I know the victory will one day be won.

I need more ammunition to take this demon down.
I'm pleading for your help to cover every ground.
Send up a word of prayer- let's call out our children's name.
We place each and everyone of them in our Savior's hand.

James 5:16b- The effectual fervent prayers of the righteous availeth much.

Celebrate-Don't Player-Hate

Every time I get on the computer, I get this awful stare.
The look upon his face says, "why are you sitting there?"
Like I do not have the right to touch this instrument.
I believe he has forgot that it was paid for by my hard earned cents.

I'm the one that paid this bill from the very start.
All I asked of him was for him to do his part.
For months he sat upon his seat and did not share in the load.
Now he has the nerve to curse at me, I thinks that very bold.

The time has come to celebrate not to player hate.
He had the chance to do the same but he choose to procrastinate.
I feel the spirit of jealousy is now attacking me.
Coming from the one within- this just should not be.

The Great Pretender

What's behind that title that you've placed upon yourself?
Strutting with your head up high and the Bible laying on the shelf.

Doing your best to paint a picture that all in life is well.
When all along you know deep within everything is going to hell.

Why on earth can't you be real and tell the truth my friend.
Why live a lie from day to day and continue to live in sin.

Telling people on the job something that you're not.
Oh my friend take off the mask and end this senseless plot.

I just can't seem to comprehend why you play these games?
One day the truth will blow up in your face and who will be the blame?

Picture Perfect

One day I had this dream of how I thought my life should be.
A picture-perfect life so full of love and other things.
A life so full of happiness so that I would never have to frown.
Boy did my bubble burst with so many ups and downs.

A marriage made in Heaven I thought mine was sure to be.
I received a rude awakening the day he laid his hands on me.
The next time I married a preacher and I was so proud as I could be.
Till one night after a Christmas party,
He was brought home drunk as he could be.

The picture-perfect family was all I wished to see.
Then I had four sons and I was awakened to reality.
I came in early from work one day happy as I could be,
Then walked in on a son who was sitting in the dark and smoking
weed.

My picture-perfect world came crushing down on me.
When two of my teenage sons took my life to a new degree.
In and out of the courtroom I found myself overtime.
I wondered how I got there? This dream could not be mine!

A picture-perfect world, this just cannot be.
It's only in a dream and not in reality.
No picture-perfect world do you think I will ever see?
The picture-perfect world is only a fantasy.

One Cold Shot!

The question was asked the other night
"Pastor where's your wife?"
The next time I hear those words-
I might not be polite!

Another women looked at me and asked,
"How dumb can that person be?
I had told them who I was-
When I took that seat.

I recall a while back in the restraint there I sat-
The waitress approached and asked those words
Of a woman she had missed.

He was with a female Pastor and could not see no harm.
But to others looking in- they only saw the charm.
All I could do was sit and stare and wait for his response,
Although it might have been innocent-
It really did cause some harm.

Talking about your good being evil spoken of-
This is sure a fact.
We should stop and take a moment before we decide to act.

Another Lie

Another lie I heard today
"I will do it your way."
Just as soon as I turned my head,
I looked around to the same old dread.
Always talking a very smooth talk
But when it's all done- you need to walk.
Telling lies after lies to hide the truth,
Have you forgotten it will come back at you?
Then you stand before me looking so dumb.
The truth now out and you're starting to hum.
Humming the same tune day after day,
One lie after another-is that your way?

What Happened to the Family?

It used to be a happy home with laughter everywhere.
Now I stare at empty walls and silence beyond compare.
There was a time when we stood as one.
Now all we do is fuss, fight, and destroy the common bond.
What Happened to the Family?

What happened to the family when what was said
Stayed within the house.
Now it is shouted from the rooftop and spread from mouth to mouth.
What happened to the family, is ringing within my soul.
I'm trying so hard to understand those stories grandmother told.
Stories of love, laughter and harmony were these all just a fact.
Or was it just a story to see how we would react.
What happened to the family.

What happened to the family when the husband took the lead.
He provided for his home and mentored to such a degree.
The wife stood in submission and carried out her part.
The children honored their parents and cherished them from the start.

What happened to the family that has caused the man to leave.
Wandering in a world of sin because he decided not to cleave.
The women now raising the children and struggling from day to day.
The children speaking out in defiance and don't cat about what they
say.
What happened to the Family!!!

What happened to the family did we move God out of the way?
Did we get so educated that we forgot just how to pray?
Did we forget about the vows we made to God and then our spouse?
Did we let our guards down and allow other things to sprout??
What Happened to the Family!!!

In the Midst of the Pain

The pain within my heart is so hard to comprehend.
As I look upon my family and the state I find them in.
Picking up the things that they see laying around .
Can't understand the meaning of stealing,
On this my heart does frown.

I taught them right from wrong from the time that they were young.
The message went in one ear and came right out the other.
Their actions speak out loud and clear that they were not listening to
their mother.
They just can't seem to comprehend the pain that I now feel.
The consequences of their choices is certainly not a thrill.

I've asked myself so many times where did things go wrong.
I just can't understand why they chose to leave my home.
I've poured out my soul from day to day to keep them out of danger.
Now many years upon this earth and they treat me like a stranger.

The questions ring out like a song from the morning into the night.
The answers will one day appear to me and all will look so bright.
So in the midst of the pain I will continue to pray and express
myself through poems.
For the Father knows and He does care and I will rest within His arms.

Right or Wrong

When right is wrong and wrong is right I can not understand.
You try to do the things that's right but still get kicked in the chin.

Trying so hard to understand what a relationship is to be.
You pour into it your very best but still get knocked down to your knees.

I was taught that the men should lead his family by the hand.
All I see is him leading himself and his family left on the sand.

I try so hard to payback the wrong that has been done.
But I can't do railing for railing, it's not my place to harm.

Am I just plan stupid for feeling the way I feel?
I just don't understand this relationship even be for real.

Live the Teaching

Stand strong my friend and don't be wrong.
You must live the life and live the song.
You talk the talk from day to day.
Others are watching you along the way.

I hear what you said but I saw what you did.
Look at the message you sent my friend.
Double tongued and living a lie,
Look out my friend your words just died.

Live the teaching that you speak.
Reach out my friend to the soul that's weak.
They just don't listen to what you speak-
They see exactly what you teach!!

Just Be Real

Realize we are living in the last days,
Our lights need to shine in every way.
Somebody out there is watching you
Please be real and live the truth.

We can stand tall and talk the talk.
But what ever happened to walking the walk.
Why do we stagger and straddle the fence?
Can't we stand tall and just be for real?

The Bible says, "the way of the transgressor is hard."
So why live a lie and sow discord.
We are a light shining upon a hill.
Our life is a witness so just be real.

No matter what you are going through,
Just keep it real Jesus is here to help you.
No one likes anything that is fake,
So just be real for Christ sake!!!

In Search of a Father's Love

Searching for a father's love and a hand to hold.
Don't know which way to go in a world so cold.
Searching for a father's love in this world below.
Questions coming from all around are drowning within their soul.

Depression is sinking in and telling them that you don't have the time.
They only want to hear you speak -
to their troubled minds.
Please take the time to listen to your sons reaching out to you.
You just might have the solution to help them make it
during these perilous times.

A mother can only tell them how to be a man.
You are the main example to model out this plan.
They are growing up quickly and don't know which direction to take.
They are seeking for your attention so they won't make so many mistakes.

Please listen to them closely and read between the lines.
Take just one moment and give them a little bit of your time.
Wrap your arms around them and show them that you care.
They are searching for your love.
So please don't leave them in despair.

Peace Shall Prevail

There's a peace from the Father above,
that prevails within this house.
It's past our understanding and we just
can't figure it out.

We know that it is the enemy's job,
to kill, steal and destroy.
But the Father promised us peace-
This we can enjoy.

His peace shall prevail,
We know that this is true.
His peace is ever calming and it's
There for me and you.

No matter how loud the thunder roars
Or how the storms may blow.
His peace will prevail within this house
For our Lord is in control.

Am I Asking for Too Much?

I guess I was asking for too much
When I asked the members to move to one side.
I began to hear murmuring and whispering
Why was I wasting so much of their time.

I guess I was asking for too much
When I asked "Did you pay that bill?"
I want to keep my money too
And spend it at my own will.

I guess I was asking for too much
When I asked, "Can you help me with the Load?"
Is your hands broken too
So you can't help me clean and fold?

I guess I was asking for too much
When I asked you to help ease my pain.
The load would be so much lighter
And we both will have something to gain.

Am I asking for to much...????

I Send You Angels

I send angels to you my dear friend.
To minister you peace and strength within.
To guard you from all of the hurt and pain.
To give you shelter in the midst of the rain.

I send angels to you- you are special you see.
That's why the enemy is attacking thee.
You must pass this test so please stay strong.
Run safely my dear child into the Savior's Arms.

I send angels to speak life to thee.
"You shall Live and not Die"-you will see.
This storm you are in is only a test.
Pray to the Father and He will give you rest.

*Psalm 34:7 The angel of the Lord encampeth round
about them that fear him, and delivereth them.

I'm Throwing A Party

It's time to throw a party.
So please don't be late.
I want to throw a tantrum,
And break up all the plates.

This is a very special party,
No Birthdays- Showers- or Teas.
I'm throwing a Pity-Party,
And no one is invited but me.

I'm moping over ill treatments-
That you have given me.
The money you will not give me,
And the attention I want shown to me.

I do not need cake or ice-cream,
neither balloons or punch you see.
For I'm throwing a Pity-Party-
For all the world to see.

At the Crossroad
(Triolet)

I'm standing at the crossroads one more time
Waiting in the meantime where do I go
Longing to hear a word from the Divine
I'm standing at the crossroads one more time
Praying for answers while in the meantime
Father above let the finances flow
I'm standing at the crossroads one more time
Waiting in the meantime where do I go

Psalms 34:6 This poor man cried,
and the Lord heard him,
and saved him out of his troubles.

Forgive Me Please

Forgive me please for my sharp tongue.
I didn't realize I was doing harm.

Forgive me please for offending you.
I was hurting when I lashed out at you.

Forgive me please for wounding you.
I spoke to quick and this is true.

Forgive me please- my dear friend.
I don't want to stay in sin.

*We must forgive one another so our
Heavenly Father will forgive us also. Mark 11:25

Pass or Return

I just can't seem to comprehend
The lessons life brings.
While traveling on this journey
All I want to do is sing.

I hear singing in my spirit
As I walk from day to day.
But I see a different agenda
Written upon my slate.

Sometimes things happen and all
I want to do is cry.
Then I do my best
To understand the reasons way!

Other times it feels like I'm on a roller coaster
Going up and down.
I laugh sometimes, cry sometimes, and
May even wear a frown.

One thing is for certain-
There is a lesson that must be learned.
I must pass this test or
This lesson will return.

No Pity-Parties Allowed

Fix your face my dear child.
It's time for you to put on a smile.
Lift your head and don't you cry.
This pity-party has got to die.

Playing sad songs all day long.
Rehearsing matters that have gone wrong.
Time to change to a brand new tune.
Sing a new song and stop playing the blues.

Your Father knows just what you need.
He also sees your every deed.
So do not worry my dear child.
Your Father will reward you so please-
Smile…

His Strength

By His strength and mercy, I have passed another test.
No man can take the credit.
Through His guidance I've done my best.

All Glory goes to my Dear Father above.
Day by day I have walked in His unconditional love.
When I became weak, His words have made me strong.
I hid them within my heart, so I could rest within His arms.

His mighty hands have guided me every step of the way.
Through these storms of life, I have certainly learned how to pray.
I pray for His wisdom to help me through each test.
I pray for the answers so that I can do my best.
I pray for strength and courage so I can lay my head down and rest.

Oh the Choices That We Make

Many roads we walk upon in this barren land.
Even made many choices that wasn't always grand.
We must learn by all our choices that we make from day to day.
We laugh a lot, we cry a lot, and we even learn how to pray.

We stand at life's crossroads wandering which way to go.
Many roads out there pulls at us to the very core.
We try so hard to choose the right path we must take.
But sometimes in our choosing we still make many mistakes.

We need you Lord to hold our hand as we journey down here below.
Without your strength and guidance we just don't know where to go.
Only you know the destiny that you have ordained for all of our life's.
We need your very leading so we can choose to do what's right.

I Must Forgive

It has not been easy
facing life storms.
For all the wrong you have ministered
has caused me so much harm.

Many, many nights
I just could not sleep.
All the pain and anguish has caused
my heart to weep.

Through the midst of every storm
there was a lesson to be learned.
Even though I felt
This pain I did not earn.

Through the tears and all the pain
I know I must forgive.
I must release all of my pains to God
For this is the Father's will.

Within the House

Wounded within the house-
And no one could even see.
Wounded within the house-
This just should not be.

Wounded within the house-
Can't you hear the screams?
Wounded with the house-
Who could be so mean?

Wounded within the house-
I'm bleeding internally.
Wounded within the house-
I will take it to eternity.

Wounded within the house-
I need healing deep within.
Wounded within the house-
Can you please help me to live again?

Can You Hear Me?

Can you hear me now?
Can you hear me now?
Or am I praying Lord to low?

Can you hear me now?
Can you hear me now?
Questions are drowning within my soul.

Can you hear me now?
Can you hear me now?
Lord I need to know-
I need answers to these questions,
And I don't know where else to go!

Psalm 61:2 From the end of the earth will I cry unto thee,
when my heart is overwhelmed:
lead me to the rock that is higher than I.

Help Me Not to Faint
(Anaphoric)

Lord in this state of pandemic-
Help me not to faint.
Standing at the crossroad one more time-
Help me not to faint.
Living in isolation now.
Help me not to faint.
The world's crying out "I can't breath"-
Help me not to faint.
Church doors are closed around the world.
Help me not to faint.
We're praying now-Lord Heal Our Land-
Help me not to faint.
Needing you as never before-
Help me not to faint.

How Long?

How long must one continue to fight?
Going through changes night after night.
Searching for answers day after day.
Convincing yourself they are on there way.

How long must one's heart continue to bleed?
Fighting with a son's addiction to weed.
Staying away from home night after night.
Will a poor mother lose this fight?

How long must a mother fight back the tears?
Struggling in a relationship year after year.
Trying to find her way out of the slumps.
Constantly running into bump after bump.

"How long must I wait?"
I heard the preacher say.
Till my change come one of these days.
My breakthrough is coming this I do see.
I will hold fast to all that is promised to me.

Help Me to Understand

Lord help me to understand all the pain I feel inside.
Wounds cut down so deep I just want to hide.
Trying to understand why do I feel the way I do.
The people don't understand why they have cut me half in two.

My Father knows the reason why I feel this way.
I must turn it all over to Him- He's only a prayer away.
So step by step I will walk this road.
Even If I have to cry.
Each day will get much better- All I have to do is try.

All it takes is a little faith.
Cultivate it Day by Day.
Trust the savior's Leading.
He will lead you every step of the way.

And Who Will Pray?

While listening to the comments of others looking in-
I kept hearing this question- Who Will Pray for Them?
Who will stand within the gap for those you love so much?
Will others constantly pray for them, or will they just give up?

Who will burn the midnight oil and go God in Prayer?
Who will pray for your loved ones that does not have a care?
Who will pray for their protection each and every day?
Who will ask for ministering angels to guide them along the way?

Who will push back their plate and give up that awesome meal?
Who will war with Satan for him to take his hands off of them?
Who will perform the task that God has instructed for me to do?
I will pray and pray until I get that final breakthrough!!

Longing to Hear

Even if I did not take it
I would still love to hear
The advice of my dear mother
Oh how I wish she was near.
I would love to pick up the phone
And hear her voice at the other end.
The kind words of my mother
Brings comfort to the confusion within.
During the storms of life
She helps me to weather every storm.
Oh how I long to be near my mother
And rest safely within her arms.
It's during these times of struggles
Oh how I miss her so much.
Years and Years of her teaching
It certainly pulls at the heart
To hear her words of wisdom
It keeps pulling my heart apart.

Oh Destiny

Moving about from day to day
Trying to understand why things are this way.
Needing to understand the state that I'm in.
Is it fate or am I reaping a past sin.

Destiny oh destiny is leading me-
Even on a path that is hard to see.
Yet I do my best to understand.
The destiny that is written in the Lord's plan.

Challenges are facing me from day to day.
At times I find it so hard to pray.
Buried down deep I pull out a song.
Even when others are doing me wrong.

Destiny oh destiny where will you lead?
Through more pain or through more grief?
The answers I may never know-
But I feel "Oh Destiny" is pulling at my soul.

When God Is Silent

When God is silent, and I do not hear Him speak.
My heart inside is aching and I feel so weak.
I began to wonder did I do something wrong.
Are my prayers even reaching up to His mighty throne?

When God is silent it is so hard for me to bear.
Is my Savior listening? Does He even care?
Not seeing the outcome of the circumstances all around.
My head drops down low and I begin to frown.

When God is silent no answers can be found.
I pray and pray much harder, but I feel like I'm losing ground.
Even from the scriptures I read, read, and read.
Yet I can't seem to comprehend the lines to such a degree.
My mind becomes so blank when His voice I do not hear.
Searching and searching for answers causes my heart to fear.

Oh when God is silent my heart begins to weep.
My spirit becomes so broken, and I fall down at His feet.
I give my burdens to Him one tear at a time.
Although He does not answer- I know He is on the line.

Psalm 28:1 Unto thee will I cry, O Lord my rock: be not silent to me:
Lest, if thou be silent to me, I become like them that go down into the
pit.

We All Have a Cross to Bear

No need to worry, no need to fear
About all that I'm going through.
Everyone has their cross to bear and
That also includes you.
Your cross my not be the same as mine
But yet you must go through.
You must also bear your cross
Regardless of what others say or do.

Into our lives some rain must fall
Or how else would things grow?
We need the water from day to day
To wash within our soul.

No need to worry I've past my test
No matter how hard it seemed.
I've put my trust in a living God
He knows the beginning and end to all things.
He knows exactly what lies ahead and
The detours I must take.
I will follow His leading and guidance
For in Him there are no mistakes.

The Way We Were
(Acrostic)

Twins walking together for 63 years.
Heart to heart we felt each beat.
Eternal twinship that will never end.

When we were together we thought as one.
Always agreeing to disagree.
Your voice I hear in my spirit now.

Wishing you were still by my side.
Each day passes my thoughts are of you.

We will be back together one day.
Entertaining each other with a heavenly song.
Rejoicing with the saints up above.
Embracing you with love once again.

In Memory of my twin: Martha Walker (Left)
Sunrise: 08/31/1957-
Sunset: 12-22-20

Not As Planned
(Rhyming Couplets)

My Heart has been torn in two.
O dear God help me make it through.

This moment is not what I planned.
I did not get to hold your hand.

Hearing this sad news makes me cry.
I had no time to say goodbye.

I never pictured it this way.
All I can do right now is pray.

Pandemic has us sheltered in.
This feels like a horrible sin.

Although we are miles apart-
This family is in my heart.

My twin Martha is now at rest.
Her life is free from all the stress.

Our dear Father has called her home.
I hear him say "Servant Well Done."

We can Make our plans, but the Lord determines our steps.
Proverbs 16:9

Not A Cheerful Christmas (Quatern)

Not a cheerful Christmas this year.
Lost a love one who was so dear.
The family mourns on this day.
My dear "Twin" has passed away.

This pandemic has all in fear.
Not a cheerful Christmas this year.
The news has torn my heart apart.
We were together from the start.

Twins hold a special bond you see.
She's always been a part of me.
Not a cheerful Christmas this year.
Martha has always been so near.

My spirit really feels so numb.
To sickness she has overcome.
I'm trying to hold back the tear(s).
Not a cheerful Christmas this year.

Forever In My Heart
(Triolet)

Twin in my heart you will always be.
Precious memories I see on today.
Thoughts of you will truly be close to me
Twin in my heart you will always be.
From sickness and pain you are now set free.
Memories I'll hold in a special way.
Twin in my heart you will always be.
Precious memories I see on today.

Needing to Hear
(Triolet)

We walked together for sixty-three years.
I didn't realize it would be this hard.
These last few days has been filled up with tears.
We walked together for sixty-three years.
How I long to hear your Voice in my ears.
Your sudden passing sure took me off guard.
We walked together for sixty-three years.
I didn't realize it would be this hard.

Flowing Tears
(Triolet)

The tears of sorrow continues to flow.
Loss of my twin has torn my heart apart.
Looking at your picture I see a glow.
The tears of sorrow continues to flow.
Knowing you're absent I will miss you so.
The tears of sorrow continues to flow.
Loss of my twin has torn my heart apart.

If Only I Could
(Anaphora/Whitney)

If only I could tell you-
Of the pain I feel inside.

If only I could tell you-
Maybe this pain would subside.

If only I could tell you-
How this sorrow has bruised my heart.

If only I could tell you-
Your departure has torn my world apart.

My heart aches-
As days go by.
Tears I shed-
Because of you.
My God knows-
I miss you so.
Twin forever in my heart.

We are living in a day and time when life is being cut so short. Please let go of the grudges and mistake of the past. We can agree to disagree and move on. Do it while you can so you don't live in a world of regrets.

Longing For You
(Lilibonelle)

Oh Father above this is hard.
My twin passed without a goodbye.
No longer asking how are you?
Time after time I need to cry.

My twin passed without a goodbye.
I often wonder what went wrong.
The pain sure does linger inside.
Losing you I try to stay strong.

No longer asking how are you?
I'm finding it hard not to call.
Daily wanting to hear her voice.
Recording of you-I'll recall.

Time after time I need to cry.
The tears do flow and that's no doubt.
Forever you'll be in my heart.
In the meantime your name I'll shout!

Through These Tears of Love

Focusing through these tears of Love.
Spending time with my twin above.
In my heart I do miss so-
Wondering why you had to go.

Thoughts of you I can't get rid of.
Focusing Through these tears of love.
I miss calling you on today
In my room now- I sit and pray.

I'm praying you were here right now
But Father-God would not allow.
Focusing through these tears of love
The times we shared I will speak of.

This day will just not be the same
I will truly call out your name
Birthday greetings I will write of
Focusing through these tears of love.

Rest in Heave Martha Kay Walker
8-31-1957 - 12-22-2020

Celebrating Through Tears
(Triolet)

Through tears of love I celebrate today.
My first birthday alone without my twin.
During the pandemic she passed away.
Through tears of love I celebrate today.
Lonely without you on this special day.
Trying my best to find comfort within.
Through tears of love I celebrate today.
My first birthday alone without my twin.

Rest in Heaven Martha Kay Walker
08-31-1957-12-22-2020
Forever in my Heart

A Word of Thanks

I just want to thank you
For taking this journey with me.
It was not always easy
Sharing my pains you see.
I have learned this journey was not about me
But "Him."
God will get the glory
Although the journey at times was grim.

Thank you- thank you- Thank you
For reading line by line.
By writing out these poems I know
I will find healing in time.
So in the meantime
I will bring this journey to an end.
You have allowed me to share
"My Side"
Now I can rest in "Him."

Other Books By This Author:

Healing Through Poetry

Publish America.com: ISBN: 1-60672-770-2

        Hard Copy ISBN: 1-4489-1407-8

In the Midst of the Storm

        ISBN: 978-0-557-97943-1

        Hard Copy ISBN: 978-1-4583-4254-6

Spiritual Breakthrough with Poetry

        ISBN: 978-0-557-83260-6

From Out of the Pit I Cried

        ISBN: 978-0-557-12237-0

Poetry With A Twist

        ISBN: 978-1-105-02781-9

        Hard Copy ISBN: 978-1-105- 04868-5

Remembering Mama's Prayers

        ISBN: 978-1-257-90642-0

        Hard Copy ISBN: 978-1-257-95905-1

On Broken Pieces-Sweat and Tears-

        ISBN: 978-1-257-376-93-3

        Hard copy ISBN: 978-257-37693-3

Duhart's Expressions Writing With Style

        ISBN: 978-0-557-28948-6

Life's Attitude

ISBN 9781300672944

Undercurrents of the Soul

ISBN 9781312622692

An Attitude of Praise

ISBN 9781300051374

Hard Copy ISBN: 9781300118671

Invisible Tears

ISBN: 9781105593048

Hard Copy: ISBN 9781105634079

14: Seasons of My Life

ISBN: 9781105340024

Hard Copy: ISBN 9781105440441